Preface

A big snakehead fish I saw in the stream when I was eight.
A chestnut looking like a diamond that I picked up when I was little.
The sunset I watched with my father.
The smell of the sea.

They say that people, even when they get old, never forget the memories and habits from their childhood because they experience them directly through their five senses.

Animals have a homing instinct, which leads them to their home, nest or birthplace. Maybe we also have something similar to a homing instinct that makes itself felt in our lives – even when we are living in countries with different cultures and lifestyles.

This book provides an insight into how Japanese people of different ages and occupations live their lives, embracing their memories, drawing from what they experienced directly through their five senses.

Takao Kitayama

序文

8歳の頃に小川で見た大きな雷魚。
子供の頃に拾ったダイヤモンドのような栗。
親父と見た夕日。
潮のにおい。

人間は10歳までに五感を通して体感した様々な記憶や習慣を、歳をとっても忘れないといいます。

動物が自分のすみかや巣、生まれた場所へ帰ってくる本能的な性質を帰巣本能といいますが、文化や生活様式の異なる国での、わたしたちの生活においても、同じようなことがいえるのではないでしょうか。

この本では、年令や職業の異なる日本人が、文化、風習の異なる国でも、五感を通して体感してきた記憶を大切にしながら生活する様子が見えてきます。

北山孝雄

About "Japanese Rooms"

How do the Japanese live in Japan? How do they live abroad? Do they create their own culture in foreign cities? What do they take with them from home? Feelings, things – sensuous or tangible memories?

Having lived in Japan for two and a half years himself, the artist and graphic designer Sven Ingmar Thies gained insight into the lives of 82 Japanese citizens in five global cities over the course of nine years:

- Tokyo
- Vienna
- New York
- Shanghai
- Berlin

Through his discreet observation he manages to capture fleeting moments of everyday Japanese life at home and abroad. He depicts the living spaces of a very diverse group – from architects to students, from business people to chefs to artists.

Using analogue black-and-white photography, Sven Ingmar Thies combines the subjects' blurred motions with classic stills of the rooms they live in.

「日本人の部屋」について

日本人は日本でどのような暮らしをしているのだろうか。海外ではどうだろう。見慣れぬ都市で自分たちの文化を作ろうとするのだろうか。日本からは何を持っていくのだろう。気持ち、物、感覚的な記憶、それとも実体のある記憶?

アーティストであり、グラフィックデザイナーでもあるスフェン・イングマー・ティースは日本に2年半暮らした経験を元に9年間に渡り、5つの国際都市で生活する82人の日本人の生活の様子を追った。

・東京
・ベルリン
・ニュー・ヨーク
・上海
・ウィーン

入念な観察を通じ、日本や海外で暮らす日本人の日常生活の一瞬を捉えた写真である。建築家、学生、芸術家、料理人からビジネスマンにいたるまで非常に多岐に渡るグループの生活空間が紹介されている。銀塩のモノクロ写真を使用し、不鮮明に写る住人の動きと、居住空間の古典的なスチール画像を組み合わせている。

Tokyo					東京

Hair stylist (30), 30 years in Tokyo   美容師（30歳）東京在歴30年

What is in your fridge right now?
Yogurt, milk, seasoning, chocolate, vegetables, fruit and typical Japanese food made from soybeans: natto, tofu and tofu milk, etc.

How long do you commute to work and how many hours do you work there every day?
Lecturer at a private university, three days a week, approx. seven hours altogether. Commuting time: two hours per day.

Which thing in your appartment/flat/house reminds you of Japan the most?
Tatami floor, iron tea kettle for tea ceremony, bamboo blind.

What do you like about the city you live in?
It is convenient in the sense of...
  ...good transportation system at the closest station Nerima: there are two underground lines (Oedo-Line and Yurakucho-Line) and one private railway line (Seibu-Ikebukuro-Line), which take us to any part of Tokyo.
  ...there are several supermarkets that offer us good prices.
  ...the ward office, central post office, library etc. are nearby.

What is your favourite spot in your place?
Sunny balcony facing to the south.

How much do you spend on rent, and how many square meters do you have?
No rent – I own both small flats, each approx. 36m^2.

Lecturer in geography (58), 58 years in Tokyo

今現在、冷蔵庫の中にあるものは何ですか？
ヨーグルト、牛乳、調味料、チョコレート、野菜、果物、納豆、豆腐、豆乳　等々、

一日平均あたりの通勤時間と勤務時間を教えてください。
私立大学講師、週3日ほどの勤務（週7時間位）、通勤時間は2時間

あなたのアパート・マンション・家の中にあるもので自分にとって一番日本を思わせるものは何ですか？
畳、茶釜、すだれ

あなたの住んでいる町の好きなところ（理由）は何ですか？
便利なところ、...
  ...大江戸線と有楽町線の地下鉄が2本と、私鉄の西部池袋線が近くの練馬駅を通っているので、どこに行くにも便利
  ...スーパーマーケットがいくつもあるので、値段も競合していて消費者に有利である
  ...区役所、中央郵便局、図書館などが近くにある

あなたの住んでいるアパート・マンション・家で気に入っているスポットはどこですか？
日当たりの良い南向きのバルコニー

あなたのアパート・マンション・家の広さ(m2)と家賃は？
購入したアパートなので家賃はなし。小さなアパート二軒でそれぞれ36㎡

地理学講師（58歳）東京在歴58年

Day nursery toddler (2), 2 years in Tokyo 保育園児（2歳）東京在歴2年
Designer (34), 34 years in Tokyo デザイナー（34歳）東京在歴34年
Designer (33), 15 years in Tokyo デザイナー（33歳）東京在歴15年

Housewife (73), 45 years in Tokyo   主婦（73歳）東京在歴45年

18 Economics student (24), 5 years in Tokyo   学生経済専攻（24歳）東京在歴5年

Art director (47), 40 years in Tokyo
Designer/illustrator (43), 26 years in Tokyo
Junior high school student (13), 13 years in Tokyo
High school student (18), 18 years in Tokyo

アートディレクター（47歳）東京在歴40年
デザイナー/イラストレーター（43歳）東京在歴26年
中学生（13歳）東京在歴13年
高校生（18歳）東京在歴18年

Modern dancer (23), 23 years in Tokyo　　　　　モダンダンサー（23歳）東京在歴23年

Housewife (73), 48 years in Tokyo
Guard (75), 48 years in Tokyo

主婦（73歳）東京在歴48年
警備員（75歳）東京在歴48年

Hair stylist (25), 25 years in Tokyo　　　美容師（25歳）東京在歴25年

Head of construction work (48), 48 years in Tokyo　　　　建設現場監督（48歳）東京在歴48年

Primary school student (8), 8 years in Tokyo   　　　　小学生（8歳）東京在歴8年

What is in your fridge right now?
Mugi-cha (barley tea), kimuchi (seasoned cabbage), cat food, eggs, meat, etc.

How long do you commute to work and how many hours do you work there every day?
Commuting: one and a half hours, average working hours: nine hours.

Which thing in your appartment/flat/house reminds you of Japan the most?
Fences around the house.

What do you like about the city you live in?
1. I can go out for a walk in casual clothing.
2. The city is full of things that remind me of my childhood.

What is your favourite spot in your place?
In front of my computer – as it is my hobby.

How much do you spend on rent, and how many square meters do you have?
I live with my family, so no rent. I have a 10m²-room.

Senior high school student (18), 18 years in Tokyo

今現在、冷蔵庫の中にあるものは何ですか？
麦茶、キムチ、猫のえさ、卵、肉など、

一日平均あたりの通勤時間と勤務時間を教えてください。
1,5時間 平均勤務時間 9時間

あなたのアパート・マンション・家の中にあるもので自分にとって一番日本を思わせるものは何ですか？
家の塀

あなたの住んでいる町の好きなところ（理由）は何ですか？
1. 特に意識しない服装でも外を散歩できること
2. 懐かしいものがたくさんある

あなたの住んでいるアパート・マンション・家で気に入っているスポットはどこですか？
趣味のコンピューターの前

あなたのアパート・マンション・家の広さ(m2)と家賃は？
10㎡、実家ぐらしです

高校生（18歳）東京在歴18年

Housewife (44), 18 years in Tokyo　　　　専業主婦（44歳）東京在歴18年

Fish market employee (28), 28 years in Tokyo 魚市場勤務（28歳）東京在歴28年

What is in your fridge right now?
Milk, eggs, seasoning, frozen food (fried pork), cans of beer, apples...

How long do you commute to work and how many hours do you work there every day?
No commuting time (I write and edit at home), 13 hours (trip to Kyushu to cover motorbike races).

Which thing in your appartment/flat/house reminds you of Japan the most?
Chabudai (round, low Japanese table).

What do you like about the city you live in?
My apartment is located in central Tokyo, so you can easily travel to other places. On sunny days we can see Mt. Fuji from the window facing to the west. And I live in a public housing unit, so the rent is very low.

What is your favourite spot in your place?
In front of our TV set.

How much do you spend on rent, and how many square meters do you have?
344 Euros per month, about 30m².

Primary school student (6), 6 years in Tokyo
Housewife (32), 15 years in Tokyo
Toddler (1), 1 year in Tokyo
Motorsports journalist (34), 15 years in Tokyo

今現在、冷蔵庫の中にあるものは何ですか?
紙パック入りの牛乳、卵、調味料、冷凍食品（fried pork)、缶ビール、リンゴ...

一日平均あたりの通勤時間と勤務時間を教えてください。
0時間（自宅での編集・執筆）、13時間（九州のサーキットへの遠征）

あなたのアパート・マンション・家の中にあるもので自分にとって一番日本を思わせるものは何ですか?
ちゃぶ台

あなたの住んでいる町の好きなところ（理由）は何ですか?
どこへ行くにもアクセスが便利。天気のいい日は西側の窓から富士山が見える。公営の団地なので家賃が安い。

あなたの住んでいるアパート・マンション・家で気に入っているスポットはどこですか?
テレビの前

あなたのアパート・マンション・家の広さ(m2)と家賃は?
約30㎡、32,000円

小学生（6歳）東京在歴6年
主婦（32歳）東京在歴15年
子供（1歳）東京在歴1年
モータースポーツ記者（34歳）東京在歴15年

Manager (40), 40 years in Tokyo   マネージャー（40歳）東京在歴40年

University student (20), 20 years in Tokyo　　　大学生（20歳）東京在歴20年
University student (23), 23 years in Tokyo　　　大学生（23歳）東京在歴23年

Berlin ベルリン

Tax adviser (39), 38 years in Berlin (German)
Housewife (29), 1 year in Berlin

税理士（39歳）ベルリン在歴38年（ドイツ人）
主婦（29歳）ベルリン在歴1年

What is in your fridge right now?
Yogurt, fruit, vegetables, eggs, frozen natto.

How long do you commute to work and how many hours do you work there every day?
Commuting: 20 minutes, studying: 8 hours.

Which thing in your appartment/flat/house reminds you of Japan the most?
Bamboo tea whisk.

What do you like about the city you live in?
Especially in summer I like to go to a park and read books, enjoy a picnic or barbecue with friends. I have moved several times in Berlin and I always found parks nearby. I have to read a lot of books and it gives me a pleasant feeling to read books in the shade of trees with a breeze blowing.

What is your favourite spot in your place?
My balcony.

How much do you spend on rent, and how many square meters do you have?
250 Euros, 45m².

Art history student (40), 5 years in Berlin

今現在、冷蔵庫の中にあるものは何ですか？
ヨーグルト、果物、野菜、卵、冷凍の納豆

一日平均あたりの通勤時間と勤務時間を教えてください。
通勤に20分、勉強に8時間。

あなたのアパート・マンション・家の中にあるもので自分にとって一番日本を思わせるものは何ですか？
茶筅

あなたの住んでいる町の好きなところ（理由）は何ですか？
特に夏はよく公園に行って本を読んだり、友達とピクニックやグリルを楽しみます。ベルリンで何度か引越しをしたけど、いつも近くに公園がある。本を多く読まないといけないので、木陰で風に吹かれながら本を読むのは気持ちいい。

あなたの住んでいるアパート・マンション・家で気に入っているスポットはどこですか？
バルコニー

あなたのアパート・マンション・家の広さ（㎡）と家賃は？
45㎡、35,000円

大学生、美術史専攻（40歳）ベルリン在歴5年

Artist/curator (35), 1 year in Berlin
Art journalist (37), 1 year in Berlin

アーティスト/キュレーター（35歳）ベルリン在歴1年
美術担当記者（37歳）ベルリン在歴1年

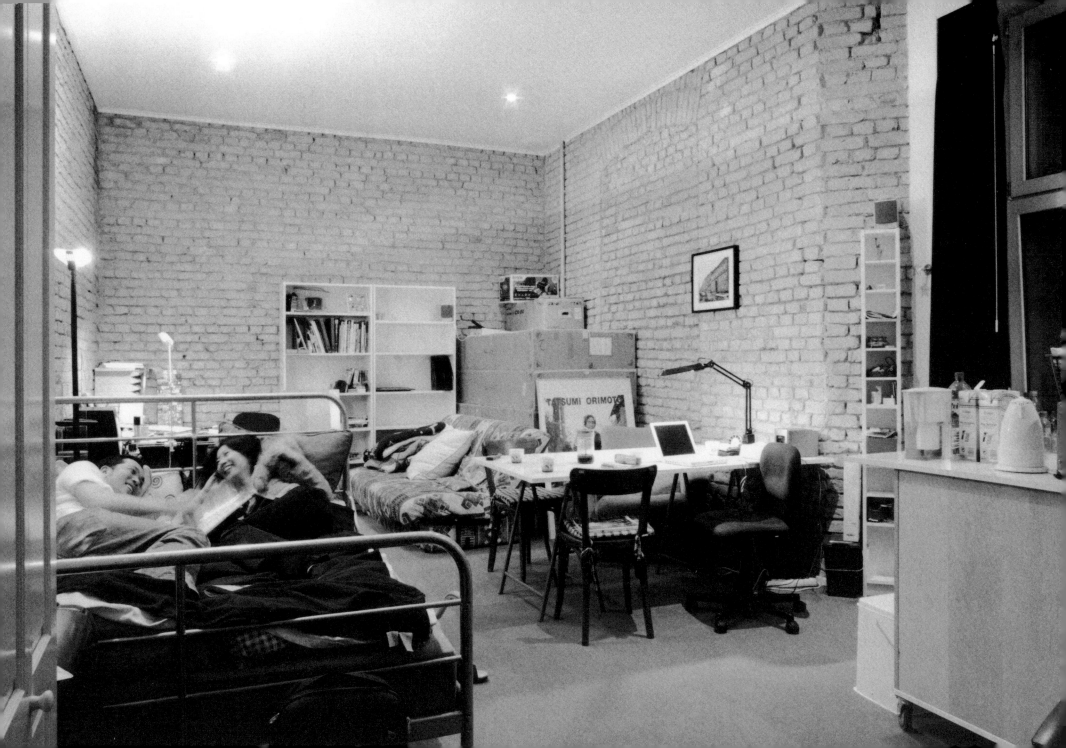

German literature student (33), 1 year in Berlin　　　大学生、ドイツ文学専攻（33歳）ベルリン在歴1年

Writer (27), 1 year in Berlin   ライター（27歳）ベルリン在歴1年

Office employee (36), 2 years in Berlin
Toddler (2), 2 years in Berlin
Student of Medicine (33), 2 years in Berlin

サラリーマン（36歳）ベルリン在歴2年
幼児（2歳）ベルリン在歴2年
医学部学生（33歳）ベルリン在歴2年

Student of meteorology (23), 1 year in Berlin   気象学科学生（23歳）ベルリン在歴1年

Art student (25), 1 year in Berlin　　　　　大学生、芸術専攻（25歳）ベルリン在歴1年

Housewife (32), 6 years in Berlin
Engineer (45), 12 years in Berlin (German)
Toddler (1), 1 year in Berlin
Child (5), 5 years in Berlin

主婦（32歳）ベルリン在歴6年
エンジニア（45歳）ベルリン在歴12年（ドイツ人）
子供（1歳）ベルリン在歴1年
子供（5歳）ベルリン在歴5年

What is in your fridge right now?
Bread, butter, cheese, beer and soybean scions.

How long do you commute to work and how many hours do you work there every day?
I live on a pension.

Which thing in your appartment/flat/house reminds you of Japan the most?
Japanese dolls.

What do you like about the city you live in?
Brandenburger Tor and Pariser Platz (the centre of Berlin where many historical incidents happened. Even today, all kinds of events take place here.

What is your favourite spot in your place?
Hallway and anteroom.

How much do you spend on rent, and how many square meters do you have?
No rent, about 500m².

Retired embassy secretary (70), 26 years in Berlin

今現在、冷蔵庫の中にあるものは何ですか?
パン、バター、チーズ、ビール、もやし

一日平均あたりの通勤時間と勤務時間を教えてください。
私は年金生活者です。

あなたのアパート・マンション・家の中にあるもので自分にとって一番日本を思わせるものは何ですか?
日本人形

あなたの住んでいる町の好きなところ（理由）は何ですか?
ブランデンブルグ門とパリー広場（そこはベルリンの中心でいろいろな出来事の舞台となった。また今も. いろいろな行事が行われる。）

あなたの住んでいるアパート・マンション・家で気に入っているスポットはどこですか?
廊下 控えの間

あなたのアパート・マンション・家の広さ(㎡)と家賃は?
約500㎡、無料

元領事館秘書（70歳）ベルリ在歴26年

Art history student (22), 1 year in Berlin　　　　　　　　美術史学生（22歳）ベルリン在歴1年

DJ/journalist (30), 6 years in Berlin	DJ/ジャーナリスト（30歳）ベルリン在歴6年

What is in your fridge right now?
Miso, soy sauce, umeboshi (plum pickles), milk, radish, eggs, mayonnaise, mustard, butter.

How long do you commute to work and how many hours do you work there every day?
10 minutes, about 5 hours.

Which thing in your appartment/flat/house reminds you of Japan the most?
Japanese dictionary.

What do you like about the city you live in?
It is multicultural here in Berlin. Different nationalities, different ideologies, different life styles are mixed. By getting to know the people, my horizons expand.

What is your favourite spot in your place?
Living room.

How much do you spend on rent, and how many square meters do you have?
340 Euros including heating and electricity, 49 m².

Artist (33), 3 years in Berlin
Artist (34), 3 years in Berlin (Romanian)

今現在、冷蔵庫の中にあるものは何ですか?
味噌、醤油、梅干、牛乳、大根、卵、マヨネーズ、マスタード、バター

一日平均あたりの通勤時間と勤務時間を教えてください。
十分、約五時間

あなたのアパート・マンション・家の中にあるもので自分にとって一番日本を思わせるものは何ですか?
国語辞典

あなたの住んでいる町の好きなところ（理由）は何ですか?
マルチカルチャーなところ。様々な国籍、様々なイデオロギー、様々なライフスタイルが混ざり合っている。色んな人と知り合うことで、自分の世界が広がる。

あなたの住んでいるアパート・マンション・家で気に入っているスポットはどこですか?
居間

あなたのアパート・マンション・家の広さ(m2)と家賃は?
49㎡、47,600円（光熱費込み）

芸術家（33歳）ベルリン在歴3年
芸術家（34歳）ベルリン在歴3年（ルーマニア人）

Lecturer in fashion design (44), 13 years in Berlin   ファッションデザイン講師（44歳）ベルリン在歴13年

Freelance curator (30), 6 years in Berlin　　　　フリーランス キュレータ（30歳）ベルリン在歴6年

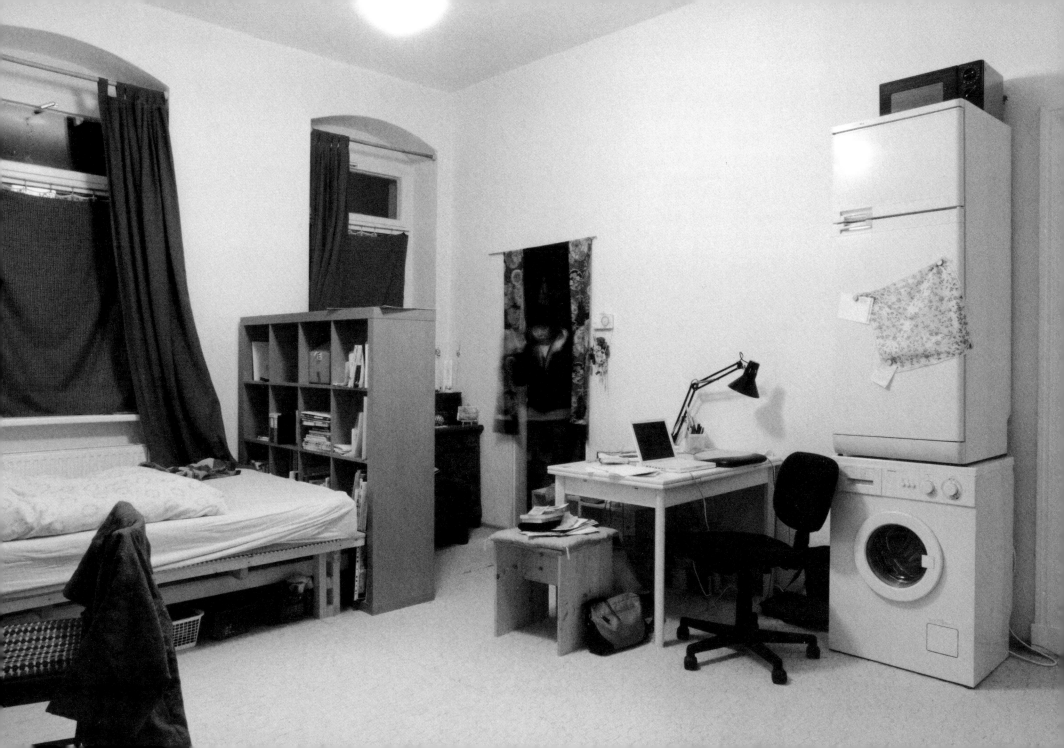

Pianist (49), 17 years in Berlin
High school student (17), 17 years in Berlin
High school student (14), 14 years in Berlin
High school student (14), 14 years in Berlin

ピアニスト（49歳）ベルリン在歴17年
学生（17歳）ベルリン在歴17年
学生（14歳）ベルリン在歴14年
学生（14歳）ベルリン在歴14年

Language student (31), 1 year in Berlin   語学生（31歳）ベルリン在歴1年

Butoh dancer/choreographer (44), 19 years in Berlin
Actor (44), 24 years in Berlin (German)

舞踏家／振付家（44歳）ベルリン在歴19年
役者（44歳）ベルリン在歴24年（ドイツ人）

Sanrio shop owner (44), 18 years in Berlin　　　　　　　　　サンリオショツプ経営（44歳）ベルリン在歴18年

Artist (57), 18 years in Berlin   美術創作家（57歳）ベルリン在歴18年

Copywriter (44), 17 years in Berlin (German)
Fashion designer (43), 18 years in Berlin

コピーライター(44歳)ベルリン在歴17年(ドイツ人)
ファッション デザイナー(43歳)ベルリン在歴18年

New York　　　　　　　　　　ニュー・ヨーク

Accounting assistant (52), 6 years in New York						会計アシスタント（52歳）ニュー・ヨーク在歴6年

Editor (33), 2 years in New York
CEO/design director (52), 25 years in New York (British)

エディター（33歳）ニュー・ヨーク在歴2年
CEO/デザインディレクター（52歳）ニュー・ヨーク在歴25年（英人）

Gallery director (36), 12 years in New York　　　　画廊ディレクター（36歳）ニュー・ヨーク在歴12年

Artist (35), 7 years in New York
Actor (35), 10 years in New York (American)

アーティスト（35歳）ニュー・ヨーク在歴7年
俳優（35歳）ニュー・ヨーク在歴10年（米人）

Attorney (42), 8 years in New York (American)
Unemployed (33), 8 years in New York

弁護士（42歳）ニュー・ヨーク在歴8年（米人）
無職（33歳）ニュー・ヨーク在歴8年

What is in your fridge right now?
Soda water, beer, champagne, milk, tofu, mekabu (seaweed), nukazuke (Japanese pickles), cheese, salami, castella (sponge cake).

How long do you commute to work and how many hours do you work there every day?
Commuting time: 20 minutes using the underground, average working hours: about 12 hours.

Which thing in your appartment/flat/house reminds you of Japan the most?
Household Shinto altar.

What do you like about the city you live in?
Anything could happen, anything is available. New York is like patchwork. Here everything is accepted as long as it works - a spirit of practicality and rationalism.

What is your favourite spot in your place?
Living room.

How much do you spend on rent, and how many square meters do you have?
We bought the apartment 5 years ago, approx. 200m².

Designer (38), 10 years in New York
Designer (35), 10 years in New York (Austrian)

今現在、冷蔵庫の中にあるものは何ですか?
炭酸水、ビール、シャンペン、牛乳、豆腐、メカブ、ぬか漬け、チーズ、サラミ、カステラ

一日平均あたりの通勤時間と勤務時間を教えてください。
通勤は、地下鉄で20分、勤務時間は大体12時間。

あなたのアパート・マンション・家の中にあるもので自分にとって一番日本を思わせるものは何ですか?
神棚

あなたの住んでいる町の好きなところ（理由）は何ですか?
何でもありなところ。ニューヨークは、パッチワークの集積でできている。とりあえず、機能すれば良いと言う功利的で合理的な精神が良い。

あなたの住んでいるアパート・マンション・家で気に入っているスポットはどこですか?
リビングルーム

あなたのアパート・マンション・家の広さ(㎡2)と家賃は?
約200㎡、アパートは5年前に購入

デザイナー（38歳）ニュー・ヨーク在歴10年
デザイナー（35歳）ニュー・ヨーク在歴10年（オーストリア人）

Frame maker (44), 5 years in New York　　　　　フレーマー（44歳）ニュー・ヨーク在歴5年

Artist (47), 14 years in New York
Artist (66), 40 years in New York
Student (12), 12 years in New York

芸術家（47歳）ニュー・ヨーク在歴14年
芸術家（66歳）ニュー・ヨーク在歴40年
学生（12歳）ニュー・ヨーク在歴12年

Cook (28), 1 year in New York   料理人(28歳) ニュー・ヨーク在歴1年

Painter (34), 15 years in New York　　　　画家（34歳）ニュー・ヨーク在歴15年

What is in your fridge right now?
So many things that I cannot write all of them down. Milk, eggs, vegetables, leftovers, natto, etc.

How long do you commute to work and how many hours do you work there every day?
About half an hour, nine hours.

Which thing in your appartment/flat/house reminds you of Japan the most?
Electric rice cooker.

What do you like about the city you live in?
Cultural diversity in every aspect. Williamsburg was originally an industrial zone with strong Italian, Polish and Hispanic communities in the north end of Brooklyn. In the 90's, many young artists moved to this neighbourhood because of the large open space, then turned it into a place people called the second Soho. Now the city's artistic flair attracts young professionals from all over the world. By just walking down the street we can encounter the most contemporary living cultures from every corner of the world.

What is your favourite spot in your place?
High ceiling.

How much do you spend on rent, and how many square meters do you have?
No rent since as we own it, about 600m².

Toddler (1), 1 year in New York
Fine artist (34), 7 years in New York
Industrial designer (33), 7 years in New York

今現在、冷蔵庫の中にあるものは何ですか?
なんでもかんでも、すべての物。牛乳、卵、野菜、納豆、残り物、などなど...

一日平均あたりの通勤時間と勤務時間を教えてください。
だいたい30分くらい、9時間

あなたのアパート・マンション・家の中にあるもので自分にとって一番日本を思わせるものは何ですか?
電気釜

あなたの住んでいる町の好きなところ(理由)は何ですか?
ありとあらゆる面における文化的多様性。Williamsburgは元々はイタリア人、ポーランド人、南アメリカ人のコミュニティーを持つブルックリンの北にある工業地帯でした。そこに広い空間を求めて90年代に芸術家達が移って来て以来この町は第二のソーホーと呼ばれるようになりました。現在、その芸術的で自由な町の雰囲気は芸術家のみならず世界中の若いプロフェッショナルたちを引き寄せています。町を歩くだけで生きた世界中の近代文化に出会う事が出来る場所です。

あなたの住んでいるアパート・マンション・家で気に入っているスポットはどこですか?
吹き抜けの高い天井

あなたのアパート・マンション・家の広さ(m2)と家賃は?
約600m²持ち家なので家賃なし。

幼児(1歳)ニュー・ヨーク在歴1年
芸術家(34歳)ニュー・ヨーク在歴7年
工業デザイナー(33歳)ニュー・ヨーク在歴7年

International civil servant (28), 4 years in New York 国際公務員（28歳）ニュー・ヨーク在歴4年

Branding consultant (39), 9 years in New York
Architect (40), 9 years in New York (American)

ブランディングコンサルタント（39歳）ニュー・ヨーク在歴9年
建築家（40歳）ニュー・ヨーク在歴9年（米人）

What is in your fridge right now?
Pasta, vegetables, water, seaweed, soybeans, beer, etc.

How long do you commute to work and how many hours do you work there every day?
10 seconds (my home and office are in the same building), 8 hours of work.

Which thing in your appartment/flat/house reminds you of Japan the most?
Telephone.

What do you like about the city you live in?
Energetic, free, beautiful, dirty, lovely – the city offers so many opportunities. Makes me excited and positive.

What is your favourite spot in your place?
High ceilings, which I look up at while lying on the bed.

How much do you spend on rent, and how many square meters do you have?
No rent, 161m².

Architect/scholarship holder (36), 2 months in New York

今現在、冷蔵庫の中にあるものは何ですか?
パスタ、野菜、水、のり、枝豆、ビールなど

一日平均あたりの通勤時間と勤務時間を教えてください。
10秒（自宅と仕事場が同じ場所）、8時間

あなたのアパート・マンション・家の中にあるもので自分にとって一番日本を思わせるものは何ですか?
電話機

あなたの住んでいる町の好きなところ（理由）は何ですか?
活気があって、自由で、美しくて、汚くて、愛おしくて、チャンスがあるところ。また、興奮させ、前向きにしてくれるところ。

あなたの住んでいるアパート・マンション・家で気に入っているスポットはどこですか?
ベッドに横たわりながら、見上げる高い天井。

あなたのアパート・マンション・家の広さ(m2)と家賃は?
161m²、家賃なし

建築家/奨学金取得者（36歳）ニュー・ヨーク在歴2ヶ月

Jewellery artist (24), 6 years in New York
Graphic designer (28), 4 years in New York

ジュエリーアーティスト（24歳）ニュー・ヨーク在歴6年
グラフィックデザイナー（28歳）ニュー・ヨーク在歴4年

Musician (36), 4 years in New York   ミュージシャン（36歳）ニュー・ヨーク在歴4年

Shanghai 上海

What is in your fridge right now?
Fruit. (I'm a vegetarian and also normally eat out.)

How long do you commute to work and how many hours do you work there every day?
Three minutes/nine hours.

Which thing in your appartment/flat/house reminds you of Japan the most?
Family photos.

What do you like about the city you live in?
There are not many foreigners around, so I am able to feel the local Chinese atmosphere very much.

What is your favourite spot in your place?
The living room where I can even do some exercise.

How much do you spend on rent, and how many square meters do you have?
330 Euros, 160m².

Director (31), 1 year in Shanghai
Law office secretary (31), 1 year in Shanghai

今現在、冷蔵庫の中にあるものは何ですか?
果物（菜食主義+ほぼ外食です）

一日平均あたりの通勤時間と勤務時間を教えてください。
3分/9時間

あなたのアパート・マンション・家の中にあるもので自分にとって一番日本を思わせるものは何ですか?
家族の写真

あなたの住んでいる町の好きなところ（理由）は何ですか?
あまり外国人が住んでいないためローカル色が強い所

あなたの住んでいるアパート・マンション・家で気に入っているスポットはどこですか?
運動もできる広いリビング

あなたのアパート・マンション・家の広さ(㎡)と家賃は?
160㎡、47,800円

ディレクター（31歳）上海在歴1年
弁護士事務所　秘書（31歳）上海在歴1年

Marketing researcher (23), 5 months in Shanghai   マーケティングリサーチャー（23歳）上海在歴5ヶ月

General manager (44), 9 years in Shanghai   部長（44歳）上海在歴9年

Hair stylist (30), 2 years in Shanghai　　　　　　　　美容師（30歳）上海在歴2年

IT manager (29), 5 years in Shanghai
Toddler (1), 1 year in Shanghai
Sales representative (27), 3 years in Shanghai (Serbian)

IT会社　副総経理（29歳）上海在歴5年
子供（1歳）上海在歴1年
営業代表（27歳）上海在歴3年（セルビア人）

President/CEO (45), 14 years in Shanghai
Vice president (51), 3 years in Shanghai

代表取締役/CEO（45歳）上海在歴14年
副社長（51歳）上海在歴3年

Illustrator (26), 3 years in Shanghai イラストレーター（26歳）上海在歴3年

Translator (Chinese-Japanese) (28), 1 year in Shanghai　　翻訳（中国語−日本語）（28歳）上海在歴1年

Designer (29), 6 years in Shanghai　　　　　　　　　デザイナー（29歳）上海在歴6年

What is in your fridge right now?
Milk, cream cheese, minced meat, bacon, cabbage, tea, tomatoes, potatoes, ice cream and figs.

How long do you commute to work and how many hours do you work there every day?
Commuting time: 20 minutes, working hours: ten.

Which thing in your appartment/flat/house reminds you of Japan the most?
A Buddha statue we bought at an antique market on the street.

What do you like about the city you live in?
Prices are low, it is exciting, the old colonial and the new glass and steel architecture of the buildings.

What is your favourite spot in your place?
Sitting on our sofa looking out of the floor-to-ceiling windows and taking in the view of the French Concession below.

How much do you spend on rent, and how many square meters do you have?
470 Euros, 130m².

Real estate manager (26), 4 years in Shanghai (American)
Executive assistant (25), 4 years in Shanghai

今現在、冷蔵庫の中にあるものは何ですか?
牛乳、クリームチーズ、ひき肉、ベーコン、キャベツ、お茶、トマト、ジャガイモ、アイスクリーム、イチジク

一日平均あたりの通勤時間と勤務時間を教えてください。
通勤時間:20分、勤務時間:10時間

あなたのアパート・マンション・家の中にあるもので自分にとって一番日本を思わせるものは何ですか?
仏像

あなたの住んでいる町の好きなところ(理由)は何ですか?
物価が安い、賑やか、古い植民地風そして現代的なグラスや鉄の建築建物。

あなたの住んでいるアパート・マンション・家で気に入っているスポットはどこですか?
リビングのソファー(後ろの大きな窓からフランス疎開の家が見える)

あなたのアパート・マンション・家の広さ(m2)と家賃は?
130㎡、64,000円

不動産マネージャー(26歳)上海在歴4年(米人)
エグゼクティブアシスタント(26歳)上海在歴4年

144 Office employee (29), 4 years in Shanghai   会社員（39歳）上海在歴4年

Trader (31), 1 year in Shanghai
University student (23), 1 year in Shanghai

商社勤務（31歳）上海在歴1年
大学生（23歳）上海在歴1年

What is in your fridge right now?
Mineral water, oolong tea, Suntory beer, butter, pickled plums, ice cubes, ice cream.

How long do you commute to work and how many hours do you work there every day?
About one hour/eight hours of work.

Which thing in your appartment/flat/house reminds you of Japan the most?
PC.

What do you like about the city you live in?
There are restaurants serving food from all kinds of countries. So I can enjoy a variety of dishes at reasonable prices. Tea plantation farmers are settling in Shanghai and all sorts of Chinese tea and information about it are available.

What is your favourite spot in your place?
A large window facing to the south, which provides a view of the ever-changing city of Shanghai.

How much do you spend on rent, and how many square meters do you have?
About 600 Euros per month, 90m².

Student adviser (30), 2 years in Shanghai
Student adviser (33), 2 years in Shanghai

今現在、冷蔵庫の中にあるものは何ですか?
ミネラルウォーター、SUNTORYのウーロン茶/ビール、バター、梅干、氷、アイスクリーム

一日平均あたりの通勤時間と勤務時間を教えてください。
約1時間、8時間労働

あなたのアパート・マンション・家の中にあるもので自分にとって一番日本を思わせるものは何ですか?
パソコン

あなたの住んでいる町の好きなところ(理由)は何ですか?
いろんな国のレストランがあってそれぞれの国の食べ物が安く食べられる。中国中の中国茶や茶農が集まってきて、茶葉や情報が手に入る。

あなたの住んでいるアパート・マンション・家で気に入っているスポットはどこですか?
変化する上海の街の様子が見渡せる大きな南向きの窓

あなたのアパート・マンション・家の広さ(m2)と家賃は?
90㎡、82,000円/月

留学アドバイザー (30歳) 上海在歴2年
留学アドバイザー (33歳) 上海在歴2年

General manager (34), 8 years in Shanghai
Secretary (29), 4 years in Shanghai (Chinese)
Toddler (2), 2 years in Shanghai
Teacher (24), visiting sister (Chinese)

部長（34歳）上海在歴8年
秘書（29歳）上海在歴4年（華人）
子供（2歳）上海在歴2年
教師（24歳）訪問中の妹（華人）

Engineer (32), 1 year in Shanghai　　　　　　　　　エンジニア（32歳）上海在歴1年

Food consultant (25), 2 years in Shanghai　　　　フードコンサルタント（25歳）上海在歴2年

Vienna　ウィーン

Artist (36), 3 years in Vienna 芸術家（36歳）ウィーン在歴3年
Artist (34), 3 years in Vienna 芸術家（34歳）ウィーン在歴3年

What is in your fridge right now?
Eggs, butter, jam, vegetables, ketchup, mayonnaise, tofu milk, toast, kimuchi, boiled rice.

How long do you commute to work and how many hours do you work there every day?
45 minutes, 6 hours.

Which thing in your appartment/flat/house reminds you of Japan the most?
Rice cooker.

What do you like about the city you live in?
The city is planned in such a way that not only tourists but also local people can enjoy their lives here.

What is your favourite spot in your place?
The view outside, sitting on the sofa in the living room and looking out of the window.

How much do you spend on rent, and how many square meters do you have?
We bought the flat, about 110m^2.

Economist (37), 1 year in Vienna (German)
Office employee (36), 1 year in Vienna
Child (4), 1 year in Vienna

今現在、冷蔵庫の中にあるものは何ですか?
卵、バター、ジャム、野菜、ケチャップ、マヨネーズ、豆乳、トースト、キムチ、ごはんですよ。

一日平均あたりの通勤時間と勤務時間を教えてください。
45分、6時間

あなたのアパート・マンション・家の中にあるもので自分にとって一番日本を思わせるものは何ですか?
炊飯器

あなたの住んでいる町の好きなところ(理由)は何ですか?
観光客はもちろんのこと、それよりも地元住人のための、地元住人が生活を楽しめる街づくりがされているところ。

あなたの住んでいるアパート・マンション・家で気に入っているスポットはどこですか?
リビングのソファから外を眺めたときにひらける窓からの景色。

あなたのアパート・マンション・家の広さ(㎡2)と家賃は?
広さ約110㎡、アパートは購入

エコノミスト (37歳) ウィーン在歴1年 (ドイツ人)
会社員 (36歳) ウィーン在歴1年
子供 (4歳) ウィーン在歴1年

Pianist (32), 1 year in Vienna
IT professional (38), 38 years in Vienna (Austrian)

ピアニスト（32歳）ウィーン在歴1年
IT専門家（38歳）ウィーン在歴38年（オーストリア人）

Artist (57), 1 year in Vienna　　　画家（57歳）ウィーン在歴1年

Opera student (26), 2 years in Vienna   オペラ学生（26歳）ウィーン在歴2年

What is in your fridge right now?
Japanese pickled plums.

How long do you commute to work and how many hours do you work there every day?
15 minutes to work, average working hours per day: 9-10 hours.

Which thing in your appartment/flat/house reminds you of Japan the most?
Family photos.

What do you like about the city you live in?
I like the classical ambience in Vienna. Also I can feel the presence of Empress Elisabeth (Sissi), whom I am very fond of.

What is your favourite spot in your place?
Window.

How much do you spend on rent, and how many square meters do you have?
650 Euros, 35m².

UN employee (32), 1 year in Vienna

今現在、冷蔵庫の中にあるものは何ですか?
うめぼし

一日平均あたりの通勤時間と勤務時間を教えてください。
通勤にかかる時間:15分
一日平均あたりの勤務時間:9~10時間

あなたのアパート・マンション・家の中にあるもので自分にとって一番日本を思わせるものは何ですか?
家族写真

あなたの住んでいる町の好きなところ(理由)は何ですか?
Sissiが大好きなので彼女を近くに感じられるこの古典的なウィーンの街の雰囲気。

あなたの住んでいるアパート・マンション・家で気に入っているスポットはどこですか?
窓

あなたのアパート・マンション・家の広さ(㎡)と家賃は?
35㎡、97,000円

国連職員(32歳) ウィーン在歴1年

Housewife (38), 3 years in Vienna
Designer (30), 15 years in Vienna (Austrian)

専業主婦（38歳）ウィーン在歴3年
デザイナー（30歳）ウィーン在歴15年（オーストリア人）

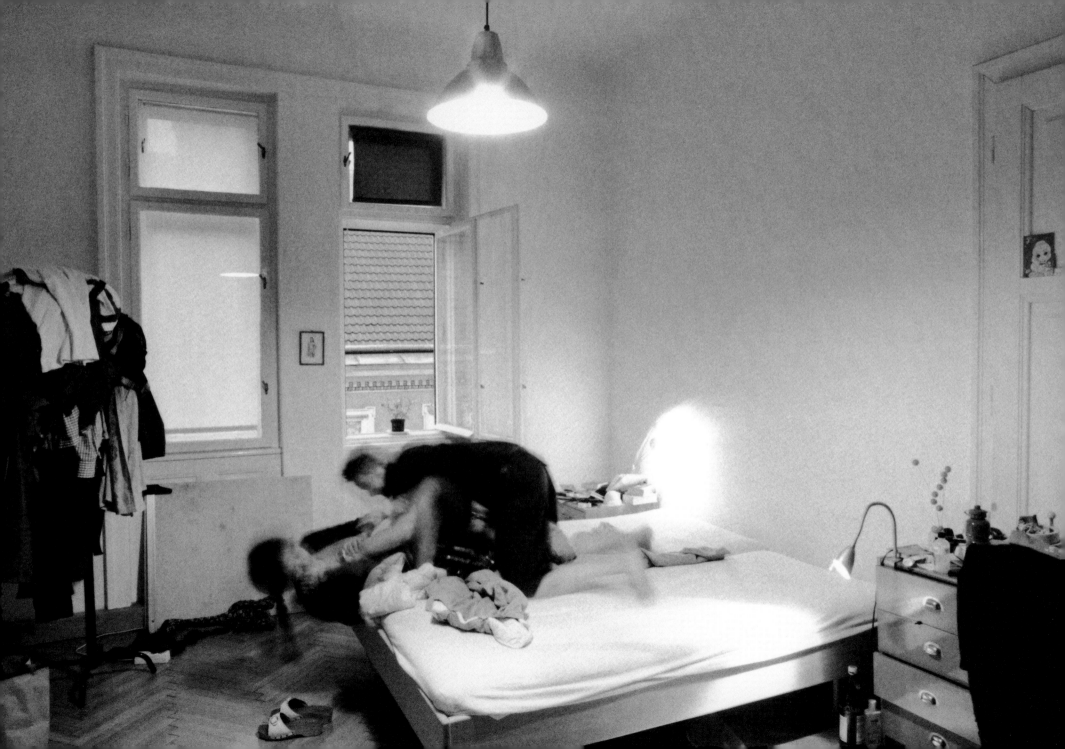

Housewife (37), 2 years in Vienna
Child (4), 2 years in Vienna
Journalist (38), 2 years in Vienna

主婦(37歳)ウィーン在歴2年
子供(4歳)ウィーン在歴2年
新聞記者(38歳)ウィーン在歴2年

What is in your fridge right now?
Beer, pork, Chinese cabbage, various Japanese seasonings.

How long do you commute to work and how many hours do you work there every day?
About 30 minutes, average working hours per day: 4 hours.

Which thing in your appartment/flat/house reminds you of Japan the most?
I don't possess things that remind me of Japan. Only when I speak with Japanese people I remember the Japanese way of thinking or its society. Thus, at home I rarely think of Japan.

What do you like about the city you live in?
It's a small city. I don't need to take a long train ride to go to a central part of the city. What I like most about this city is that, although it is small, it is very international. Here I can experience a variety of cultures and feel safe – which is rare in today's world.

What is your favourite spot in your place?
The Garden.

How much do you spend on rent, and how many square meters do you have?
350 Euros, 40m².

PhD student and secretary (42), 13 years in Vienna

今現在、冷蔵庫の中にあるものは何ですか?
ビール、豚肉、白菜、日本の調味料類

一日平均あたりの通勤時間と勤務時間を教えてください。
約30分、一日の勤務時間数は4時間

あなたのアパート・マンション・家の中にあるもので自分にとって一番日本を思わせるものは何ですか?
普段、物や出来事によって日本を思い出すことはありません。ただ、日本人と接した時に、日本の考え方、もしくは社会を思い出します。したがって、家の中では日本についてほとんど考えません。

あなたの住んでいる町の好きなところ（理由）は何ですか?
小さな町であること。市の中心まで長い時間電車に乗る必要がない。特に気に入っているのは、小さいながらも国際的な街であるというところ。居ながらにしてヴァラエティーに富んだ文化を（安全に）体験できる街は、世界の中でもあまり多くないと思う。

あなたの住んでいるアパート・マンション・家で気に入っているスポットはどこですか?
庭

あなたのアパート・マンション・家の広さ(m2)と家賃は?
40m²、50,000円

博士課程／会社秘書（42歳）ウィーン在歴13年

Energy analyst (57), 57 years in Vienna
UN employee (33), 1 year in Vienna

エネルギーアナリスト（57歳）ウィーン在歴57年
国連職員（33歳）ウィーン在歴1年

Artist (23), 1 year in Vienna　　　　画家（23歳）ウィーン在歴1年

Housewife (50), 2 years in Vienna
Nuclear engineer (56), 3 years in Vienna

主婦（50歳）ウィーン在歴2年
原子力技術者（56歳）ウィーン在歴3年

IT engineer (24), 1 year in Vienna		IT エンジニア（24歳）ウィーン在歴1年

About Sven Ingmar Thies

Sven Ingmar Thies, born in Hamburg in 1969, studied graphic design at the Braunschweig University of Art, Germany. After university he worked in London, Vienna and Tokyo.

During his two and a half year stay in Tokyo his profound interest in the Japanese way of feeling, thinking and living further intensified – and has not diminished since. For "Japanese Rooms" he spent a couple of months in each of the cities where he took photos of Japanese citizens in order to get to know the people and feel the cities' different atmospheres.

As a graphic designer Sven Ingmar Thies is specialised in branding and developing sustainable combinations of print and online media design. As an artist he primarily develops photo projects and installations – like his one-man exhibition "What Does Love Mean?" in Tokyo, 1998, or "Wave" for USM, 2007.

He lives and works in Hamburg and Vienna.

スヴェン・イングマー・ティースについて

1969年ハンブルク生まれ。ドイツBraunschweig大学 グラフィックデザイン専攻。卒業後ロンドン、ウィーン、東京でグラフィックデザイナーとして活躍。

東京で過ごした2年半で日本人の感じ方、考え方、暮らし方に深い興味を持つようになり、今だにその興味は薄れていない「日本人の部屋」では、相手をよく知り、都市それぞれに異なる雰囲気を理解できるようにするため、各都市でそれぞれ2~3ヶ月過ごして日本人の写真を撮影した。

グラフィックデザイナーとしての専門領域はブランディング及び刷媒体とオンラインのデザイン持続可能な統合。アーティストとしては写真プロジェクトとインストレーションを主とする。例としては「What Does Love Mean?」(1998年東京)、「Wave」(2007、USM)。

ハンブルグとウィーンに在住・活動。

Anne-Estelle Werner

ZIMMERMANN & PARTNER

Acknowledgments

This book has been generously supported by: Haefele Japan K.K., Tokyo (hafele.co.jp), Japan Airlines International Co., Ltd Direktion für Deutschland (de.jal.com), Patentanwaltskanzlei Anne-Estelle Werner, Industrial Property Law, Münster (aew-patent.de), and Zimmermann & Partner Patent Attorneys, Munich (zimpat.com).

謝辞

出版にあたり下記の皆様に多大なるご支援を賜りました：
株式会社　ハフェレ ジャパン、東京（hafele.co.jp）、株式会社 日本航空インターナショナル フランクフルト支店（de.jal.com）、ヴェルナーアンヌ-エステル特許事務所、ドイツのミュンスター（aew-patent.de）、ツィマーマン＆パートナー 弁理士，ミュンヒェン（zimpat.com）。

Sven Ingmar Thies
Japanese Rooms

ISBN 978-3-937623-90-0

Publisher and Distribution:
SCHWARZERFREITAG GmbH, Berlin
schwarzerfreitag.com

Editor in Chief:
Sven Ingmar Thies

Translation:
Lena Junker, Berlin
Satoko Takenoshita, Vienna

Concept and Design:
Thies Design, Hamburg and Vienna, thiesdesign.com

Image Processing:
Pixelstorm, Vienna, pixelstorm.at

Printing & Binding:
Rema Print, Vienna, remaprint.at

Paper:
Claro Bulk 150g, mapaustria.at

Copyright:
© 2007, Sven Ingmar Thies, Hamburg
All rights reserved by the editor in chief/artist. No part of this book may be used or reproduced in whatever manner without written permission of the editor in chief/artist, except in the context of reviews.

KAITEN ART

KAITENART is an art and publishing project focusing on Japanese arts and culture as well as on art in a Japanese context. It is a collaboration between: Sven Ingmar Thies and SCHWARZERFREITAG Publishing, an independent publisher. For further information please visit kaitenart.com.

カイテンアートはスヴェン・イングマー・ティースとシュワツァーフライタッグ出版社との提携により、日本のアートと文化、そして日本におけるアートに焦点をあてたアート及び出版の共同プロジェクトです。詳しくはkaitenart.comまで。